Mack F

Ellen Catala
Illustrated by Anne Catharine Blake and Doreen Gay Kassel

Rigby
A Harcourt Achieve Imprint

www.Rigby.com
1-800-531-5015

"Here, Mack," said Nell.
"You forgot your book."

"Here, Mack," said Nell.
"You forgot your folder."

"Here, Mack," said Nell.
"You forgot your boots."

"Here, Mack," said Nell.
"You forgot your coat."

"Here, Mack," said Nell.
"You forgot your hat."

"Here, Mack," said Nell.
"You forgot your umbrella."

13

"Hi, Mack!" said Nell.

"You forgot your lunch!"